Anonymous

A New System of Religion

Anonymous

A New System of Religion

ISBN/EAN: 9783337034757

Printed in Europe, USA, Canada, Australia, Japan

Cover: Foto ©Lupo / pixelio.de

More available books at **www.hansebooks.com**

A NEW SYSTEM OF RELIGION.

CHAPTER I.

THE DEITY.

O MAN, when will thy pride ceaſe to be in exact proportion to thy ignorance? When will the heavenly light of ſcience teach thee humility, and thyſelf?

Con-

Consider, ye of the human race, the various systems of religion, which have been recommended to your reverence by the tradition of your fathers. Does not one, and the same, radical error pervade them? Have not their founders taught us pride, instead of humility? Yes, ye awful fathers of our worship! ye forgot that man is but a particle of littleness, and that the Deity is infinite greatness. Ye forgot what different degrees of magnitude there are, between a grain of sand and the sun: what infinite scales of being, between the Fountain of existence and man!

Hence

Hence blaſphemous fanaticiſm has eſtabliſhed an approximation, a familiarity, between little man and the Creator of Gods. All the cares of the Deity, all the paſſions which human folly has imputed to him who is tranquillity, are concentrated in the affairs of a worm. There are no dignified beings, but the Deity and mankind; and angels, who are but the ſervants of man. Oh, horrible pride! The Deity is but a ſuperior man, in the dark conception of fanaticiſm; or men are inferior deities.

Abandon this impious familiarity, abandon it for ever, and cover

thy

thy head with duſt, thou ſon of the meaneſt exiſtence! Know that, as the particles of ſnow beneath the northern pole, as the ſand in the burning deſarts of Zaara, ſo numerous are the ſcales of ſpiritual exiſtence, between the Deity and man: and that the loweſt race of theſe beings knows that man is but the ſhadow of nothing.

Sages have conceived that, as there are venomous, and apparently uſeleſs, reptiles in the lower ſcale of exiſtence, ſo there may, in the infinite number of worlds, be ſome apparently noxious and uſeleſs; and whoſe real uſe is only known to the

Creator.

Creator. As a toad, or a viper, upon earth, ſuch may this globe be in the number of worlds. Her inhabitants may have been created, and the lunar orb appointed to maintain their native frenzy, as examples of folly to ſuperior beings, that they may, by compariſon, know the value of wiſdom, and be happy.

The intentions of the Creator we cannot know: but the pride of man we know, and the cauſe of that pride. Before the teleſcope laid open the wonders of the ſky, it was thought that the ſtars were but ornaments to our dome, and ſparks to illumine our darkneſs. But by what mental telescope shall we discover the superior scales of spiritual existence; and learn humility, by comparing ourselves with the inhabitants of eternal day? We are proud, because superior to beasts, whom we see, and know: and might be humble, could we see, and know, even the lowest link of an infinite chain of superior being.

The Atheist, and the Deist, and the worshipper of received faiths, are alike misled by pride. The Atheist erects himself into the intellectual arbiter of the universe; and thinks there is no knowledge, but what resides in his own bosom.

How

How canſt thou prove the exiſtence of a Deity, when thou canſt not prove thy own? Art thou not as fanatic, abſolutely to deny, as others, abſolutely to believe? Do not thy ſenſes, and thy reaſon, perpetually deceive thee? how then canſt thou know that there is no God? True it is that the credulity of the nations is vaſt, and the arts of prieſts various: but obſerve well the fabric of this world, and the various ſcale of being which our organs admit us to perceive, and confeſs the probability of a Deity; nay, of many ſuperior beings, of ſuch power as to be gods to mankind, though as men to the Fountain

tain of Life. Is thy mind ſo narrow, as to think that human conceptions impriſon the univerſe? Is man the only rational being, becauſe the only one with whom we are acquainted? If thou believeſt that there is no God, thou art thyſelf credulous; and if thou wiſheſt to perſuade others, thou art but a fanatic of a new faith. Atheiſt, doubt of thy faith: doubt, but do not tremble. Let not the pride of man perſuade thee, that thy opinions can excite any paſſion, but pity, in the minds of ſuperior beings.— Could a man create a fly, and put it into his garden, would he not ſmile to find, that the fly denied the existence of his creator? Would he be angry? No. He would say the eyes of a fly are but small, and how can he see a large object?

And thou, Deist, why has thy pride made thee so familiar with the Deity? Thou believest in the existence of man, and in the existence of one God; but formest no conception of the infinite distance between God and man; nor allowest that there must be infinite orders of rational being, between the meanest and the highest. The meanest of these orders must be as gods to thee; and yet thou laughest at the Polytheist.

But

But the greateſt pride belongs to the received faiths, which bring down the Deity to human littleneſs, and level him in our duſt. Syſtems of blaſphemy, when will ye ceaſe to diſgrace human reaſon! Thou, fanatic, art humble. Know that thy humility is the extremity of pride. The purple tyrant is a ſtranger to the pride that ſwells thy heart. Thou art humble with man, but the boſom friend of thy God, who hears all thy petitions; and has appointed and ſelected thee from the maſs of mankind, to be his familiar companion in this life, and in eternity.—Thou art humble!

To human pride are all religions indebted for their progreſs; and a more powerful and univerſal principle could not be employed. Hold out the idea of a ſelect, and choſen, ſociety, entitled to benefits unknown to the reſt of mankind, and you will be greedily heard. And what is this life to eternity? Let us, ſay they, be bruiſed, and humbled in this life; while even here we are ſupported with the proud idea, that we are ſuperior to the reſt of mankind, and the choſen friends of God; and that we ſhall enjoy eternal glory, and happineſs, while our enemies, nay all mankind, not of our

our ſociety, ſhall have eternal torture. How deeply are pride and malice rooted in our hearts! This is what mortals call humility!

Of the Deity man can form no idea: and perhaps even the firſt ſpiritual ſcale cannot have the ſmalleſt comprehenſion of his attributes, or mode of exiſtence. Has a worm any conception of the human mind? When we ſay that the Deity is ſelf-exiſtent, infinite, eternal, what ideas can we form of thoſe qualities? None. Let us adore him in ſilence: but never imagine that our adoration can honour the Fountain of Being.

Being. Such adoration is blaſ-phemy. Our adoration only marks us as rational creatures; and excites grateful and benevolent ideas in the mind.

CHAP.

CHAPTER II.

MATTER AND CREATION.

ALL things in exiſtence, and all modes of exiſtence, have their oppoſites. Nor can the human, or perhaps any, mind form a conception of an object, without a tacit compariſon between it and its oppoſite. What idea of light, without darkneſs? of truth, without falſehood? of good, if there were no evil? It may be ſaid, that to deny exiſtence to any object, is at ſame time to deny exiſtence to its oppoſite:

poſite: for without its contrariety nothing is known to exiſt.

Hence to deny the eternity of matter, is to deny the eternity of the Deity. He is the ſupreme opposite of matter, of chaos. As the pureſt of ſpirits he muſt have had his oppoſite, in the groſſeſt of matter, from all eternity.

Had not matter been coeternal with the Deity, he muſt have filled all ſpace with infinite purity; and it was impoſſible that any corruptible matter could be produced, in a univerſe completely filled with the divine radiance.

If

If we deny a coexiſtent ſubject, we muſt allow that the Deity is the abſolute creator of evil, which ſeems abſurd; whereas if we grant the eternity of matter, the origin of evil is accounted for, without any derogation to the Creator. For even omnipotence cannot work impoſſibilities: and it is as impoſſible to impart ſpiritual perfection to matter, as it is to make darkneſs and light the ſame.

No ancient ſyſtem of religion, or philoſophy, has ever ſuppoſed that the Deity abſolutely created matter; cauſed matter to exiſt, while nothing before exiſted except himſelf.

Even

Even in the book of Genesis, the word, translated *created*, implies merely *fashioned* or *made*, as the most skilful Hebraists agree. The Bramins, the Persians, the Phœnicians, the Egyptians, the Greek philosophers, all allowed a chaos, a mass of inert matter, coexistent with the Deity.

Atheists assert of course the eternity of matter; and their antagonists assume the opposite proposition. But the eternity of matter is indeed the strongest argument for the existence of a Deity, from that aphorism that no object exists without its opposite. This seems a law of necessity,

ceſſity, of fate, as an ancient Greek would expreſs it, that even omnipotence could not alter nor controul.

But how the pureſt of ſpirits, the Deity, could act upon groſs and inert matter, it is impoſſible to conceive. Light, which is almoſt a ſpiritual ſubſtance, acts in a kind of creative capacity upon groſs matter; but that a pure ſpirit could have no contact, nor influence whatever, upon matter, is a grand argument of modern atheiſm.

The views of atheiſm are, however, as confined, as thoſe of fanaticiſm. We muſt believe that there

are

are at leaſt as many degrees, and ſorts, of ſpirit, as of matter. The creation of ſpirits by the Deity, is inconceivable by us; and perhaps even by the pureſt ſpirits themſelves. But grant that the Creator only immediately formed the Gods, the ſpirits next to himſelf in power and dignity, and imparted to them a ſupreme portion of his own creative power, why might not they either act upon matter themſelves; or by creating inferior ſpirits, but ſtill of vaſt power, miniſter to a progreſs, that led down by degrees to the creation of matter? What a vaſt idea muſt it give us of the great Firſt Cauſe to ſuppoſe even this

this world, and man, but the work of one of his remote miniſters! But can we have too vaſt ideas of the Deity? Yes, ſays human pride, we may!

CHAP.

CHAPTER III.

THE GODS.

THE polytheiſm of all ancient nations was founded upon miſtaken principles. Their gods were the offspring of human pride, and often but deified men; ever ſimilar in paſſions, and vices, to mankind their creators, not their creation. The vaſtneſs of the univerſe was unknown, even to the ancient philoſophers. This earth was eſteemed the eſſence of creation, man in the

the next degree to the gods. All religions have ſtood upon human pride.

The polytheiſm here to be eſtabliſhed, is on the contrary founded upon the vaſtneſs of the univerſe, the inſignificance of this earth, and of man. Even inferior ſpirits muſt be as gods to man, in power, in knowledge, in every attribute.

But by the Gods are here meant ſpirits of vaſt and ſuperior power; capable of creating worlds, and of annihilating them, as a man builds a houſe, and throws it down.

That

That ſuch high beings are, is inferable from the chain of exiſtence, obſervable in the material world. Nor can any idea be more honourable to the Deity, than to ſuppoſe that the ſpirits of his own immediate creation are of amazing power, and perfection, and yet inferior to him in an infinite degree. Now, if we allow the exiſtence of a Deity, the moſt magnificent ideas concerning him muſt infallibly be the moſt true.

It is probable that each God preſides over a world of his own creation, and has miniſtering ſpirits, to manage different departments. Some ancients believed that each

nation

nation had it's guardian divinity; nor can he who believes a firſt cauſe of order, think that even human affairs, little as they are, can be entirely left to human management.

If even monarchs be approached with awe, and a ſort of adoration, there can ſurely be no offence in the worſhip of the Gods, our creators and protectors. Humility, and propriety concur to dictate that our adoration of them cannot be offenſive to the Deity, whom we moſt highly honour in honouring his immediate miniſters.

Nor let the trite argument againſt polytheiſm be here applied, namely that there cannot be but one being omnipotent, and omnipreſent. This is true of the Deity, the great firſt cauſe. But man is little; and many are the beings who are gods to him. Nor can the power, or will, of theſe beings claſh. They are created pure intelligences, for good, and not for evil; and feel immediately the conſtant preſence of the omnipotent, and omnipreſent, Deity.

CHAPTER IV.

THE GENII.

THE ſpiritual orders of being are unknown to us; and of conſequence we have no diſtinct terms, even for the grand diviſions of theſe orders. A thouſand names could not expreſs even theſe grand diviſions of ſpirits, diſtinct in power, and in qualities.

The higheſt order is that of the Gods. The loweſt that of the Genii, or dæmons.

Ancient

Ancient philoſophers, who aſſerted that every human being has his guardian Genius, might with leſs abſurdity have aſſerted that every ape has his guardian man. Philoſophy is often but the quinteſſence of human pride.

The Gods cannot be evil, becauſe ſupreme intelligence, and ſupreme goodneſs, are the ſame; and wickedneſs and folly are ſiſters. But of the dæmons, whoſe mind exceeds that of man by only one degree, it is not improbable that ſome may be bad. Their forms may even partake of matter, and yet be what men may call ſpiritual. There may

be

be degrees of matter ſo fine as to eſcape our organs. The air almoſt eſcapes them.

The offices, and enjoyments, of theſe ſpirits, we are ſtrangers to; but it is highly probable that they often intermix in human affairs, and produce thoſe ſingular events, which are by ſome imputed to fortune, and by others to a ſpecial providence.

CHAPTER V.

ORIGIN OF EVIL.

IF, ſay the Atheiſts, you take away any of the attributes of the Deity, you deſtroy his exiſtence, for a Deity without benevolence, or without power, is no Deity. Granted. But evil muſt have got into the univerſe, either with the permiſſion of the Deity, in which caſe he is not all-good, or in other words, you deſtroy his exiſtence: or elſe againſt his permiſſion, in which caſe he is not

not omnipotent, and you alſo deſtroy his exiſtence: this dilemma ſeems the chief baſis of atheiſm.

But the origin of evil may be accounted for in two ways; neither of which derogates from the belief of a Deity.

The eternity of matter the Atheiſts will grant; and, without this being allowed, it ſeems impoſſible to account for the origin of evil.

Though the Deity have infinite benevolence, and infinite power to exert that benevolence, yet he cannot operate abſolute impoſſibilities.

He

He cannot make a body be in one place, and in another, at the ſame inſtant; nor can he render oppoſite objects identically the ſame. He cannot make light darkneſs, nor truth falſehood. Neither can he make matter perfect, and free from evil; which is in it's eſſence imperfect, and full of evil.

In another point of view, if pride would permit us to ſuppoſe it poſſible that this our world, and man, are but the works of inferior agents of the Deity, whoſe infinite purity could not act upon matter, the origin of evil may be partly owing to theſe agents being neither all-good

nor

nor all-powerful. And yet no imputation refts upon the Deity, any more than when we allow that the Deity made man, and yet fee how imperfect the works of man are. That the Deity can act upon matter may be an impoffibility; but it is a certain impoffibility that he can impart infinite benevolence, or infinite power, to any other being.

The eaftern dogma of an evil deity, coeternal with the good, is inadmiffible. An evil deity is a contradiction in terms. Evil feems a mere defect, or abfence of good; as darknefs is the abfence of light. Now a defect can never be an active

principle.

principle. Moral evil is the fruit of imperfect understanding; but infinite intelligence is essential to the idea of a deity.

Nor can a spirit of any superior order ever mistake evil for it's good, or in other words, be evil. The purity of it's essence must act, as a quick instinct, against evil; and the vastness of it's intelligence must guard even against it's distant approach. It is denied that evil at all exists, except in matter and material beings.

Even in human society good must exceed evil, else that society could

not

not exiſt. In all countries, and ages, a bad man is an exception to ſociety, and not a rule. An action muſt have great goodneſs to excite praiſe; and ſmall wickedneſs will incur diſpraiſe. When a man does well, he is not praiſed, becauſe he barely does what is expected; but if ill, he is blamed. The natural ſtate of man muſt be good: but man in a ſtate of perfection is a contradiction in terms, irreconcileable even by human pride.

CHAPTER VI.

MAN.

WHY am I here? ſays the Atheiſt. Thou art here, as part of a large plan, which thou canſt never conceive, nor perhaps minds of a thouſand times thy powers.

Man forms the medium between material and ſpiritual exiſtence. His component parts are perhaps the moſt diſſonant; and his character of courſe the moſt eccentric of all beings.

Some

Some fix upon one predominant character for mankind; others upon others. Some will have all men influenced only by self-interest; others by vanity. But every one needs but consult his own breast, to find that he is influenced by a variety of motives.

All mankind have indeed a leading character, namely incongruity.

The greatest minds often act, and speak, meanly; the wisest, foolishly.

Nay, the most opposite qualities are often found in the same man; the greatest folly in some respects,

joined

joined with the greateſt wiſdom in others: and the like.

Man is in ſome matters a ſpirit, in others a beaſt. If any rational being have occaſion for the utmoſt humility, it is man: and yet he is certainly of all rational beings the moſt proud. The reaſon is, that he is of all theſe beings the moſt ignorant.

CHAPTER VII.

HIS DUTIES.

THE great duty of man is to be uſeful, and beneficial to others. A noxious plant produces poiſon; a beneficial one fruits. Such is man.

The duty which we owe to the Gods is a remote, and feeble, incentive to conduct. Our more immediate motive is the good opinion of others; and a regard to the order of ſociety.

Human

Human nature has been represent-ed as in a ſtate of the utmoſt depra-vity; but it's depravity has never been ſuch, and never will be ſuch, that good actions will paſs for bad, and bad for good. Virtue lives.

Our regard for the opinion of others therefore does honour to human nature, and to it's Creator.

But, independently of the opinion of others, a man ought to do what, from the nature and eſſence of morality, he knows to be juſt and right.

Man

Man has certainly a moral inſtinct, which gives him ſatisfaction, when he does what is right; and checks him when he acts amiſs. This moral inſtinct is what is commonly called conſcience.

Moral inſtinct is as neceſſary to human exiſtence, as natural inſtinct is to that of beaſts.

This moral inſtinct is an actual emanation of the Deity, enlightening all rational minds; as the emanation of ſolar light illumines natural objects. The clouds of vice may obſtruct, but cannot extinguiſh, it.

Even brutal inſtinct is an emanation of the Deity; but as the recipient of light is, ſuch is the colour and nature of that light. A vegetable only grows by the ſolar heat: an inſect grows, and moves. The intellectual light of the Deity is alike varied, in various recipients.

Perhaps the moſt approximate motive to human action is, the eaſe and delight we feel in doing good, and our pain in doing evil.

CHAPTER VIII.

HIS HAPPINESS.

PLEASURE cannot be happineſs, becauſe conſtant pleaſure ceaſes to be ſuch.

Pleaſures demand intervals; and the higheſt of them are momentary. Happineſs muſt be conſtant; muſt exiſt in the intervals of pleaſure.

Mere eaſe, or indolence, is not happineſs, any more than ſleep is happineſs.

Happineſs

Happineſs conſiſts in the active purſuit of ſome great object; and in intervals of pleaſure and of eaſe.

The improvement of the mind is the moſt important of human purſuits; and the gradual acquiſition of virtue and of knowledge, leads to the greateſt happineſs.

If the moral inſtinct be much clouded, and the love of virtue and uſeful knowledge obliterated, the man may have many pleaſures, but never can have happineſs.

If human exiſtence terminate not with this life, it is of the laſt im-

portance

portance to preſerve the moral inſtinct clear; for in proportion to the clearneſs of that inſtinct, muſt our future happineſs be.

That vice and miſery are the ſame, is not a metaphor, but a ſimple truth. Every act of vice ſoils the mental mirror of happineſs.

CHAP.

CHAPTER IX.

A FUTURE LIFE.

MAN has no authentic title to a future life. Think not, vain mortals, that if ye died as the beaſts, the juſtice of the Deity could be arraigned. Impious thought!

Let the good be often miſerable, and the bad often happy in this life, what is it to the juſtice of the Deity? Can he work impoſſibilities,

bilities, or overcome the imperfection of matter?

Man is ſo important in his own eyes! But if he does right, what merit has he to entitle him to eternal happineſs?

Our horror at annihilation, and our ſtrong hopes of immortality, have been adduced as arguments for our immortality. Wiſe arguments! Are our fears, and wiſhes, rules for our Creator?

Could apes flatter themſelves that they ſhould at their death become men, would we regard their vain

vain imaginations, as the rules of nature?

If the ſoul be immortal, it is the effect of the goodneſs of the Creator, and not of his juſtice.

It is impoſſible to prove the immortality of the ſoul; and impoſſible to prove its mortality. But probability is in favour of the firſt poſition. For man is the being who connects the material and ſpiritual chain. As ſuch he muſt have ſomething ſpiritual in him; and what is ſpiritual cannot die.

The

The happineſs, or miſery of a future life muſt conſiſt in the ſtate of the mind. Vice muſt miniſter its own torments; virtue its own happineſs.

END.

www.ingramcontent.com/pod-product-compliance
Lightning Source LLC
Chambersburg PA
CBHW031810090426
42739CB00008B/1238

* 9 7 8 3 3 3 7 0 3 4 7 5 7 *